NOVENA TO OUR LADY OF LOURDES

Nine Days of Miracles: Journey with Our Lady of Lourdes, Embracing Prayer, Healing, and the Divine Power of Spring Water.

Theresa H. Bryan

DEDICATION

Dedicated to the pilgrims of faith and seekers of miracles, may this novena guide you on a transformative journey with Our Lady of Lourdes. May your prayers be a source of healing, and may the divine power of spring water accompany you on the path of spiritual renewal over these nine days.

Table of content

BIOGRAPHY OF OUR LADY OF LOURDES.

Our Lady of Lourdes:
A Divine Presence in Lourdes, France

Unveiling the Title

The designation "Our Lady of Lourdes" (French: Notre-Dame de Lourdes; Occitan: Nòstra Senhora de Lorda) stands as a sacred title dedicated to the Virgin Mary. Esteemed by the Roman Catholic Church, this veneration is rooted in the apparitions that transpired in the serene town of Lourdes, France.

The Extraordinary Apparitions

On the momentous day of 11 February 1858, Bernadette Soubirous, a mere 14-year-old, experienced the inaugural apparition. In the quiet confines of Massabielle's cave, located 1.5 kilometers from the town, Bernadette recounted encountering a celestial "Lady" while gathering firewood with her sister and friend. This celestial presence manifested itself on 18 occasions that year, culminating in a revelation where she identified herself as "I am the Immaculate Conception." This divine encounter captured the attention and reverence of many.

Ecclesiastical Endorsement

On 18 January 1862, the local Bishop of Tarbes Bertrand-Sévère Laurence officially endorsed the veneration of the Blessed Virgin Mary in Lourdes, affirming the authenticity of the apparitions and solidifying the town's significance as a sacred pilgrimage site.

Our Lady of Lourdes:
A Testament in Stone

Location and Witness

The sacred site, nestled in Lourdes, France, witnessed the profound encounters between Saint Bernadette Soubirous and the Blessed Virgin Mary from 11 February to 16 July 1858. The cave of Massabielle became the hallowed ground where these celestial dialogues unfolded.

Marian Apparition and Papal Approval

Recognized as a Marian apparition, the events at Lourdes gained papal approval from Pope Pius IX, who, on 1 February 1876, granted a decree of canonical coronation to the image as Notre-Dame du Saint Rosaire. The coronation, carried out by Cardinal Pier Francesco Meglia on 3 July 1876 at the Rosary Basilica, further solidified the sanctity of Our Lady of Lourdes.

Patronage and Feast Day

Our Lady of Lourdes extends her patronage over various regions, including Lourdes, France, Quezon City, Tagaytay, Daegu, South Korea, Tennessee, Diocese of Lancaster, and Lourdes School of Mandaluyong. Her feast day, celebrated on 11 February, marks a significant occasion for devotees worldwide.

The Everlasting Image: A Symbol of Devotion

Canonical Coronation and Replication

Pope Pius IX's decree not only sanctified the image but also paved the way for its widespread replication. The image of Our Lady of Lourdes has become a revered icon, finding a place in shrines and homes, adorning garden landscapes with a symbol of divine grace.

Canonization of Saint Bernadette

In 1933, Pope Pius XI canonized Bernadette Soubirous, elevating her to sainthood. This act affirmed the sanctity of her experiences and the spiritual significance of the apparitions at Lourdes.

A Growing Center of Pilgrimage

Marian devotion has flourished over the years, drawing the faithful to Lourdes for spiritual solace and miraculous intercession. The construction of a significant church at the site has solidified Lourdes as a major center for religious pilgrimage, attracting believers from all corners of the globe.

In the heart of Lourdes, the echoes of divine encounters persist, inviting pilgrims to partake in a spiritual journey marked by devotion, healing, and the enduring legacy of Our Lady of Lourdes.

The Celestial Encounter at Massabielle Grotto: A Divine Revelation

A Tranquil Day Turned Sacred

On the serene day of 11 February 1858, Bernadette Soubirous, accompanied by her sister Toinette and neighbor Jeanne Abadie, set out to collect firewood near the Grotto of Massabielle. Little did she know that this ordinary task would soon be transformed into a sacred encounter that would reverberate through the annals of spiritual history.

Mystical Signs Unveiled

As Soubirous, standing at the water's edge, removed her shoes and stockings to wade through the gentle stream, the air around her carried whispers of an otherworldly presence. Despite the stillness of the trees and bushes nearby, she heard the ethereal sound of two gusts of wind. In this mystical setting, a wild rose in a natural niche within the grotto began to move, unveiling the unseen forces at play.

The Divine Revelation Unfolds

Returning towards the grotto and in the process of taking off her stockings, Soubirous experienced a profound moment. The atmosphere resonated with the sound of a gust of wind once again, and as she raised her head, a vision unfolded. A lady dressed in white, adorned with a white dress, a blue girdle, and a yellow rose on each foot, stood before her. The beads of her rosary mirrored the color of the roses. From the dark alcove behind the niche emanated a dazzling light, illuminating the sacred space with divine radiance.

A Trembling Gesture and an Invitation

Overwhelmed by the celestial spectacle, Soubirous attempted to make the sign of the cross, but her hands trembled in awe. The lady, acknowledging her presence, smiled with grace and extended an invitation. "Pray the rosary with me," she beckoned. A divine communion was offered, transcending the earthly realm.

Secrets Unveiled and a Trial of Faith

Struggling to contain the sacred encounter, Soubirous initially attempted to keep the vision a secret. However, the bond between sisters proved unyielding, as Toinette shared the mystical revelation with their mother. Parental cross-examination ensued, resulting in corporal punishment for the two sisters—a testament to the challenges faced when trying to convey divine encounters in a skeptical world.

A Test of Holiness

Undeterred, Soubirous returned to the grotto on 14 February, armed with holy water—a symbolic test of the apparition's origin. With steadfast determination, she threw the holy water towards the lady, proclaiming that if she came from God, she should stay, but if not, she must depart. The lady responded with a smile and a bow, affirming the divine nature of the encounter. This marked the second chapter in the unfolding revelation at Massabielle Grotto—a testament to faith overcoming trials and doubt.

Triumph Amidst Trials: Bernadette Soubirous and the Miraculous Grotto

Awe and Fear in Ecstasy

As Bernadette Soubirous continued to commune with the heavenly apparition at Massabielle Grotto, her companions were gripped by fear at the sight of her ecstatic states. Undeterred, she remained in a state of divine connection even as they retraced their steps to the village.

Divine Instructions and Unwavering Faith

On 18 February, Soubirous shared a profound message from the Lady, urging her to return to the Grotto over the next two weeks. The apparition conveyed a crucial insight, stating, "The Lady only spoke to me the third time... She did not promise to make me happy in this world, but in the next." This revelation marked a turning point, emphasizing spiritual rewards over worldly contentment.

Defying Parental Warnings

Despite parental admonitions to refrain from returning to the Grotto, Soubirous, driven by unwavering faith, defied their orders. On 24 February, the Lady's message took a new direction, emphasizing the importance of prayer and penitence for the conversion of sinners—a divine call to spiritual transformation.

The Unveiling of the Sacred Spring

The subsequent revelation on 25 February instructed Soubirous to dig in the ground and drink from the emerging spring. Though this act initially left her disheveled, it led to the discovery of a stream that would become a transformative focal point for pilgrimages. Despite the initial murkiness, the waters gained a reputation for miraculous healing.

Miraculous Healings and Controversy
Word of the sacred waters spread rapidly, and numerous reports of miraculous cures surfaced. Professor Verges, in 1860, confirmed seven cures as lacking any medical explanations. However, not all claims stood the test of scrutiny, with some turning out to be short-term improvements or even hoaxes. This led to heightened concerns from both the Catholic Church and government officials.

Government Intervention and Controversial Fencing
In response to the escalating controversy, the government fenced off the Grotto, imposing strict penalties for those

attempting to access the off-limits area. Lourdes became a national issue in France, prompting Emperor Napoleon III to intervene and order the reopening of the Grotto on 4 October 1858. The church, cautious of the controversy, chose to distance itself from the unfolding events.

Divine Declarations and Miraculous Demonstrations

Undeterred by the barricades, Soubirous, guided by her intimate knowledge of the local terrain, managed to visit the Grotto under the cover of darkness. On 25 March, a pivotal declaration resounded: "I am the Immaculate Conception" ("que soy era immaculada concepciou"). Easter Sunday, 7 April, witnessed a miraculous display as Soubirous, in ecstasy, held her hands over a lit candle without harm.

The Final Pilgrimage

On 16 July, Soubirous made her last pilgrimage to the Grotto. In a testament to the enduring beauty of the divine encounters, she remarked, "I have never seen her so beautiful before." This poignant moment marked the culmination of a spiritual journey that had captivated the hearts of believers and skeptics alike.

A Vision in Humility: Bernadette's Portrayal of the Divine Encounter

The Young Girl of Grace

Bernadette Soubirous, in recounting her celestial encounter at Massabielle Grotto, described the apparition as a "jeune fille" or young girl, aged around 14-15 years. Emphasizing a connection beyond age, Soubirous insisted that the apparition stood no taller than herself. With her diminutive stature of 1.40 meters (4 ft 7 in), Soubirous found herself in the presence of a heavenly figure, bridging the earthly and divine realms.

A Garment of Purity

The heavenly visitor, as envisioned by Soubirous, was adorned in a flowing white robe, accentuated by a blue sash cinched at the waist. This attire resonated with the uniform of the Children of Mary, a religious group to which, due to her poverty, Soubirous was initially denied entry. However, the divine encounters led to her eventual admission, transcending earthly limitations. Intriguingly, her aunt Bernarde was already a devoted member of this revered religious community.

The Discrepancy in Stone

The statue enshrined in the niche of Massabielle Grotto, crafted by Lyonnais sculptor Joseph-Hugues Fabisch in 1864, serves as a visual emblem of Our Lady of Lourdes. Yet, it deviates from Soubirous' intimate depiction. The statue portrays a figure that is not only older and taller than the young girl envisioned by Soubirous but aligns more closely with conventional representations of the Virgin Mary in orthodox traditions.

Profound Disappointment in Stone

Upon encountering the statue that now stands as an iconographic symbol of Our Lady of Lourdes, Soubirous experienced profound disappointment. The disparity between her personal vision and the sculpted representation revealed the inherent challenge of translating divine encounters into tangible forms. The statue, though revered by many, failed to capture the essence of the celestial manifestation that had left an indelible mark on Soubirous' soul.

In the unfolding narrative of Massabielle Grotto, the incongruity between personal visions and external representations stands as a poignant reminder of the ineffable nature of divine encounters and the challenges of translating them into earthly forms.

Springs of Healing:

Lourdes Water and Divine Devotion

Divine Guidance to a Sacred Spring

On 25 February 1858, an ethereal encounter between Bernadette Soubirous and Our Lady of Lourdes unveiled a sacred spring, marking a pivotal moment in the spiritual narrative of Lourdes. Following the celestial directive, thousands of pilgrims have journeyed to Lourdes, heeding the instruction to "drink at the spring and wash in it," seeking solace and healing in the waters sanctified by the divine connection.

Lourdes Water: A Source of Spiritual Devotion

Lourdes water has evolved into a focal point of devotion to the Virgin Mary. The Catholic Church, while not establishing it as dogma, has formally endorsed the practice of sick individuals bathing and visiting Lourdes in search of healing. Since the apparitions, numerous claims of miraculous cures have emerged from those who have imbibed or immersed themselves in the sacred waters. Lourdes authorities generously provide this water free of charge to all who seek its potential transformative effects.

Analyzing the Waters of Grace

In 1858, then-mayor of Lourdes, Monsieur Anselme Lacadé, commissioned a thorough analysis of the spring's water. A professor in Toulouse conducted the examination, determining that the water was potable. The analysis unveiled a composition comprising oxygen, nitrogen, carbonic acid, carbonates of lime and magnesia, trace elements of carbonate of iron, an alkaline carbonate or silicate, chlorides of potassium and sodium, traces of sulphates of potassium and soda, traces of ammonia, and traces of iodine. Essentially, the water was deemed pure and inert.

A Dream of Therapeutic Springs

Monsieur Anselme Lacadé harbored hopes of harnessing the potential mineral properties of Lourdes water to transform the town into a spa destination, competing with neighboring spa towns like Cauterets and Bagnères-de-Bigorre. While the therapeutic aspirations were not fully realized in the realm of traditional spa development, Lourdes water, infused with spiritual significance, continues to draw pilgrims seeking not just physical healing but a profound connection to the divine.

In the convergence of spiritual devotion and natural elements, Lourdes water stands as a testament to the enduring interplay between faith and the tangible, where the sacred spring becomes a conduit for both physical and spiritual restoration.

Embracing Holiness:

Sanctuary of Our Lady of Lourdes

A Spiritual Haven Amidst Apparitions Situated in the heart of Lourdes, France, the Sanctuary of Our Lady of Lourdes stands as a testament to the divine encounters that unfolded in 1858. Owned and overseen by the Roman Catholic Church, this sacred expanse encompasses a rich tapestry of churches, religious edifices, and places of worship. It beckons millions of pilgrims annually, drawn to venerate the revered Our Lady of Lourdes.

Devotion and Care for the Afflicted
Beyond its architectural splendor, the sanctuary serves as a hub for devotional activities, administrative offices, and a haven for pilgrims, especially those grappling with illness. The compassionate embrace of the sanctuary extends to providing accommodations for the sick and their attendants, recognizing the intertwined nature of physical and spiritual healing.

Grotto of Massabielle: A Celestial Encounter
At the heart of the 52-hectare sanctuary lies the Grotto of Massabielle, where the young Bernadette Soubirous is said to have beheld the ethereal presence of the Virgin Mary. This sacred site, surrounded by three basilicas—the Upper Basilica,

the Lower Basilica, and the Underground Basilica—stands as a profound reminder of the divine intersecting with the earthly.

A Tapestry of Devotion and Ritual

The sanctuary's expansive grounds host a myriad of sacred spaces, including chapels, a calvary atop a hill, and open areas for communal gatherings. The intricate network of alleys serves as pathways for processions, weaving together the collective faith of pilgrims. Fountains generously provide Lourdes water, inviting seekers to partake in its spiritual essence, while baths offer immersion for those seeking both physical and spiritual renewal.

Residences of Compassion and Healing

Within this sacred precinct, residences cater to the specific needs of sick and disabled pilgrims, offering a space of respite and care. The offices of the

Lourdes Medical Bureau stand as a testament to the intertwining of faith and medical understanding, a nod to the holistic approach embraced by the sanctuary.

A Global Pilgrimage Destination
Year after year, millions embark on a pilgrimage to Lourdes, transforming the town into a global pilgrimage destination. Among the throngs are large numbers of sick pilgrims, their journey fueled by a hopeful anticipation of either physical healing or a profound spiritual reawakening.

In the convergence of celestial history and contemporary devotion, the Sanctuary of Our Lady of Lourdes stands as a sacred tapestry, weaving together the threads of faith, compassion, and healing for all who seek solace within its hallowed grounds.

The Significance of Novena

To Our Lady of Lourdes.

Embracing Divine Intercession

The Novena to Our Lady of Lourdes holds profound significance as a devotional practice seeking the intercession of the Blessed Virgin Mary. This nine-day period of prayer and reflection is a spiritual journey that intertwines the faithful with the heavenly grace associated with the apparitions at Lourdes.

Nine Days of Miraculous Devotion

The novena unfolds over nine consecutive days, symbolizing a period of anticipation and dedication. Each day becomes a sacred opportunity for believers to draw closer to Our Lady of Lourdes, expressing their hopes, supplications, and gratitude through a structured series of prayers.

Journey with Our Lady of Lourdes

As participants engage in this extended prayerful observance, they embark on a symbolic journey with Our Lady of Lourdes. The novena provides a framework for reflection on the virtues exemplified by the Virgin Mary, including purity, humility, and unwavering faith. It becomes a spiritual pilgrimage, fostering a deeper connection with the divine.

Healing, Prayer, and Divine Intervention

A central theme of the novena revolves around healing—both physical and spiritual. Believers often bring their afflictions, ailments, and challenges to Our Lady of Lourdes, seeking her compassionate intercession for recovery and solace. The novena encapsulates a profound belief in the transformative power of prayer and the divine willingness to respond to the pleas of the faithful.

Communal and Personal Devotion

The communal aspect of the novena enhances its significance, as groups of believers often gather to share in this collective spiritual experience. Yet, it also holds deep personal meaning, allowing individuals to address their unique intentions and concerns in the sacred space of prayer.

Preparation for Feast Day Celebration

The novena traditionally culminates on the Feast Day of Our Lady of Lourdes, celebrated on 11 February. This day holds particular importance in the liturgical calendar, marking the anniversary of the initial apparition to Saint Bernadette Soubirous. The novena serves as a preparatory period, enhancing the significance of the feast day celebration.

Strengthening Faith and Trust

Through the rhythmic cadence of prayer, scripture, and reflection, the novena becomes a spiritual exercise that strengthens faith and nurtures trust in the divine. Participants often find solace and guidance in the process, fostering a sense of closeness to the Blessed Virgin Mary and a renewed conviction in the power of prayer.

In essence, the Novena to Our Lady of Lourdes is a sacred and transformative practice that invites believers into a deeper communion with the divine, fostering healing, devotion, and a profound sense of spiritual connection.

NINE DAY NOVENA PRAYERS

Day 1

Let us commence this novena, invoking the presence of the Father, the Son, and the Holy Spirit. Amen.

Mary Immaculate, Our Lady of Lourdes, a pure and chosen vessel, chosen from eternity to be the Mother of the Eternal Word, and by virtue of this title, preserved from original sin, we humbly kneel before you, just as little Bernadette did at Lourdes. With childlike trust, we pray that, as we reflect on your glorious manifestation at Lourdes, you will graciously consider our current supplication, securing a favorable response to the request for which we dedicate this novena.

Oh, resplendent beacon of purity, Mary Immaculate, Our Lady of Lourdes, radiant in your Assumption and

triumphant in your coronation, reveal to us the mercy of the Mother of God. Virgin Mary, Queen and Mother, be our source of comfort, hope, strength, and solace. Amen.

Our Lady of Lourdes, intercede for us.

Saint Bernadette, intercede for us.

Say 1: Our Father…

Say 1: Hail Mary…

Say 1: Glory Be…

Day Two

Let us commence this novena, invoking the presence of the Father, the Son, and the Holy Spirit. Amen.

Mary Immaculate, Our Lady of Lourdes, a pure and chosen vessel, chosen from eternity to be the Mother of the Eternal Word, and by virtue of this title, preserved from original sin, we humbly kneel before you, just as little Bernadette did at Lourdes. With childlike trust, we pray that, as we reflect on your glorious manifestation at Lourdes, you will graciously consider our current supplication, securing a favorable response to the request for which we dedicate this novena.

Oh, resplendent beacon of purity, Mary Immaculate, Our Lady of Lourdes, radiant in your Assumption and

triumphant in your coronation, reveal to us the mercy of the Mother of God. Virgin Mary, Queen and Mother, be our source of comfort, hope, strength, and solace. Amen.

Our Lady of Lourdes, intercede for us.

Saint Bernadette, intercede for us.

Say 1: Our Father…

Say 1: Hail Mary…

Say 1: Glory Be…

Day Three

Let us commence this novena, invoking the presence of the Father, the Son, and the Holy Spirit. Amen.

Mary Immaculate, Our Lady of Lourdes, a pure and chosen vessel, chosen from eternity to be the Mother of the Eternal Word, and by virtue of this title, preserved from original sin, we humbly kneel before you, just as little Bernadette did at Lourdes. With childlike trust, we pray that, as we reflect on your glorious manifestation at Lourdes, you will graciously consider our current supplication, securing a favorable response to the request for which we dedicate this novena.

Oh, resplendent beacon of purity, Mary Immaculate, Our Lady of Lourdes, radiant in your Assumption and

triumphant in your coronation, reveal to us the mercy of the Mother of God. Virgin Mary, Queen and Mother, be our source of comfort, hope, strength, and solace. Amen.

Our Lady of Lourdes, intercede for us.

Saint Bernadette, intercede for us.

Say 1: Our Father…

Say 1: Hail Mary…

Say 1: Glory Be…

Day Four

Let us commence this novena, invoking the presence of the Father, the Son, and the Holy Spirit. Amen.

Mary Immaculate, Our Lady of Lourdes, a pure and chosen vessel, chosen from eternity to be the Mother of the Eternal Word, and by virtue of this title, preserved from original sin, we humbly kneel before you, just as little Bernadette did at Lourdes. With childlike trust, we pray that, as we reflect on your glorious manifestation at Lourdes, you will graciously consider our current supplication, securing a favorable response to the request for which we dedicate this novena.

Oh, resplendent beacon of purity, Mary Immaculate, Our Lady of Lourdes, radiant in your Assumption and triumphant in your coronation, reveal to us the mercy of the Mother of God.

Virgin Mary, Queen and Mother, be our source of comfort, hope, strength, and solace. Amen.

Our Lady of Lourdes, intercede for us.

Saint Bernadette, intercede for us.

Say 1: Our Father…

Say 1: Hail Mary…

Say 1: Glory Be…

Day Five

Let us commence this novena, invoking the presence of the Father, the Son, and the Holy Spirit. Amen.

Mary Immaculate, Our Lady of Lourdes, a pure and chosen vessel, chosen from eternity to be the Mother of the Eternal Word, and by virtue of this title, preserved from original sin, we humbly kneel before you, just as little Bernadette did at Lourdes. With childlike trust, we pray that, as we reflect on your glorious manifestation at Lourdes, you will graciously consider our current supplication, securing a favorable response to the request for which we dedicate this novena.

Oh, resplendent beacon of purity, Mary Immaculate, Our Lady of Lourdes, radiant in your Assumption and triumphant in your coronation, reveal to us the mercy of the Mother of God.

Virgin Mary, Queen and Mother, be our source of comfort, hope, strength, and solace. Amen.

Our Lady of Lourdes, intercede for us.

Saint Bernadette, intercede for us.

Say 1: Our Father…

Say 1: Hail Mary…

Say 1: Glory Be…

Day Six

Let us commence this novena, invoking the presence of the Father, the Son, and the Holy Spirit. Amen.

Mary Immaculate, Our Lady of Lourdes, a pure and chosen vessel, chosen from eternity to be the Mother of the Eternal Word, and by virtue of this title, preserved from original sin, we humbly kneel before you, just as little Bernadette did at Lourdes. With childlike trust, we pray that, as we reflect on your glorious manifestation at Lourdes, you will graciously consider our current supplication, securing a favorable response to the request for which we dedicate this novena.

Oh, resplendent beacon of purity, Mary Immaculate, Our Lady of Lourdes, radiant in your Assumption and triumphant in your coronation, reveal to us the mercy of the Mother of God.

Virgin Mary, Queen and Mother, be our source of comfort, hope, strength, and solace. Amen.

Our Lady of Lourdes, intercede for us.

Saint Bernadette, intercede for us.

Say 1: Our Father…

Say 1: Hail Mary…

Say 1: Glory Be…

Day Seven

Let us commence this novena, invoking the presence of the Father, the Son, and the Holy Spirit. Amen.

Mary Immaculate, Our Lady of Lourdes, a pure and chosen vessel, chosen from eternity to be the Mother of the Eternal Word, and by virtue of this title, preserved from original sin, we humbly kneel before you, just as little Bernadette did at Lourdes. With childlike trust, we pray that, as we reflect on your glorious manifestation at Lourdes, you will graciously consider our current supplication, securing a favorable response to the request for which we dedicate this novena.

Oh, resplendent beacon of purity, Mary Immaculate, Our Lady of Lourdes, radiant in your Assumption and triumphant in your coronation, reveal to us the mercy of the Mother of God.

Virgin Mary, Queen and Mother, be our source of comfort, hope, strength, and solace. Amen.

Our Lady of Lourdes, intercede for us.

Saint Bernadette, intercede for us.

Say 1: Our Father…

Say 1: Hail Mary…

Say 1: Glory Be…

Day Eight

Let us commence this novena, invoking the presence of the Father, the Son, and the Holy Spirit. Amen.

Mary Immaculate, Our Lady of Lourdes, a pure and chosen vessel, chosen from eternity to be the Mother of the Eternal Word, and by virtue of this title, preserved from original sin, we humbly kneel before you, just as little Bernadette did at Lourdes. With childlike trust, we pray that, as we reflect on your glorious manifestation at Lourdes, you will graciously consider our current supplication, securing a favorable response to the request for which we dedicate this novena.

Oh, resplendent beacon of purity, Mary Immaculate, Our Lady of Lourdes, radiant in your Assumption and triumphant in your coronation, reveal to us the mercy of the Mother of God.

Virgin Mary, Queen and Mother, be our source of comfort, hope, strength, and solace. Amen. 54

Our Lady of Lourdes, intercede for us.

Saint Bernadette, intercede for us.

Say 1: Our Father…

Say 1: Hail Mary…

Say 1: Glory Be…

Day Nine

Let us commence this novena, invoking the presence of the Father, the Son, and the Holy Spirit. Amen.

Mary Immaculate, Our Lady of Lourdes, a pure and chosen vessel, chosen from eternity to be the Mother of the Eternal Word, and by virtue of this title, preserved from original sin, we humbly kneel before you, just as little Bernadette did at Lourdes. With childlike trust, we pray that, as we reflect on your glorious manifestation at Lourdes, you will graciously consider our current supplication, securing a favorable response to the request for which we dedicate this novena.

Oh, resplendent beacon of purity, Mary Immaculate, Our Lady of Lourdes, radiant in your Assumption and triumphant in your coronation, reveal to us the mercy of the Mother of God.

Virgin Mary, Queen and Mother, be our source of comfort, hope, strength, and solace. Amen.

Our Lady of Lourdes, intercede for us.

Saint Bernadette, intercede for us.

Say 1: Our Father…

Say 1: Hail Mary…

Say 1: Glory Be…

Conclusion

In concluding our sacred journey within the pages of "Novena to Our Lady of Lourdes: Nine Days of Miracles," we reflect on the profound pilgrimage of prayer, healing, and the divine power embodied in the spring waters of Lourdes. Through these nine days, we embarked on a spiritual odyssey, drawing closer to the benevolent presence of Our Lady of Lourdes.

This novena has been a testament to the enduring power of faith, guiding us through moments of reflection, supplication, and a deep connection with the divine. As we delved into the intertwined realms of spirituality and healing, we explored the significance of each prayer, the devotion to Our Lady of Lourdes, and the transformative properties of the sacred water that flows from the grotto of Massabielle.

"Nine Days of Miracles" has not merely been a journey through words; it has been an invitation to experience the miracles that unfold when faith meets devotion. Our exploration of the prayers, accompanied by the stories of healing and hope, has illuminated the path of those who seek solace and renewal in the embrace of Our Lady of Lourdes.

May the echoes of our prayers resonate beyond these pages, carrying the essence of this novena into the hearts of those who embark on their own spiritual quests. Let the healing waters of Lourdes flow into the lives of believers, offering comfort, renewal, and a profound connection with the divine.

In the spirit of Saint Bernadette, whose unwavering faith paved the way for the miraculous apparitions, we conclude this novena with gratitude for the journey we've shared. May the grace of Our Lady of Lourdes accompany you on your ongoing pilgrimage of faith, and may the divine blessings encountered here continue to manifest miracles in your life.

As we bid farewell to these pages, may the sacred journey with Our Lady of Lourdes be an enduring source of inspiration, healing, and divine connection for all who have embarked on this nine-day odyssey of prayer and miracles.